EVANGELINE
A TALE OF ACADIE

By HENRY WADSWORTH
LONGFELLOW

Illustrated by
WILLIAM
MOYERS

THE PETER PAUPER PRESS
MOUNT VERNON
NEW YORK

EVANGELINE

⋈

A TALE OF
ACADIE

PROLOGUE

This is the forest primeval. The murmuring
 pines and the hemlocks,
Bearded with moss, and in garments green, in-
 distinct in the twilight,
Stand like Druids of eld, with voices sad and
 prophetic,
Stand like harpers hoar, with beards that rest
 on their bosoms.
Loud from its rocky caverns, the deep-voiced
 neighboring ocean
Speaks, and in accents disconsolate answers the
 wail of the forest.
℃ This is the forest primeval; but where are the
 hearts that beneath it

Leaped like the roe, when he hears in the wood-
land the voice of the huntsman?

Where is the thatch-roofed village, the home
of Acadian farmers, —

Men whose lives glided on like rivers that water
the woodlands,

Darkened by shadows of earth, but reflecting
an image of heaven?

Waste are those pleasant farms, and the farm-
ers forever departed!

Scattered like dust and leaves, when the mighty
blasts of October

Seize them, and whirl them aloft, and sprinkle
them far o'er the ocean.

Naught but tradition remains of the beautiful
village of Grand-Pré.

❡ Ye who believe in affection that hopes, and
endures, and is patient,

Ye who believe in the beauty and strength of
woman's devotion,

List to the mournful tradition still sung by the
pines of the forest;

List to a Tale of Love in Acadie, home of the
happy.

PART THE FIRST

➤ I ◄

In the Acadian land, on the shores of the Basin
    of Minas,
Distant, secluded, still, the little village of
    Grand-Pré
Lay in the fruitful valley. Vast meadows
    stretched to the eastward,
Giving the village its name, and pasture to
    flocks without number.
Dikes, that the hands of the farmers had raised
    with labor incessant,
Shut out the turbulent tides; but at stated sea-
    sons the flood-gates

Opened, and welcomed the sea to wander at
    will o'er the meadows.

West and south there were fields of flax, and
    orchards and cornfields

Spreading afar and unfenced o'er the plain;
    and away to the northward

Blomidon rose, and the forests old, and aloft on
    the mountains

Sea-fogs pitched their tents, and mists from the
    mighty Atlantic

Looked on the happy valley, but ne'er from
    their station descended.

There, in the midst of its farms, reposed the
    Acadian village.

Strongly built were the houses, with frames of
    oak and of chestnut,

Such as the peasants of Normandy built in the
    reign of the Henries.

Thatched were the roofs, with dormer-win-
    dows; and gables projecting

Over the basement below protected and shaded
    the door-way.

There in the tranquil evenings of summer,
    when brightly the sunset

Lighted the village street, and gilded the vanes
    on the chimneys,

Matrons and maidens sat in snow-white caps
    and in kirtles

Scarlet and blue and green, with distaffs spin-
    ning the golden

Flax for the gossiping looms, whose noisy shut-
    tles within doors

Mingled their sound with the whir of the
    wheels and the songs of the maidens.

Solemnly down the street came the parish
    priest, and the children

Paused in their play to kiss the hand he ex-
    tended to bless them.

Reverend walked he among them; and up rose
    matrons and maidens,
Hailing his slow approach with words of af-
    fectionate welcome.
Then came the laborers home from the field,
    and serenely the sun sank
Down to his rest, and twilight prevailed. Anon
    from the belfry
Softly the Angelus sounded, and over the roofs
    of the village
Columns of pale blue smoke, like clouds of in-
    cense ascending,
Rose from a hundred hearths, the homes of
    peace and contentment.
Thus dwelt together in love these simple Aca-
    dian farmers, —
Dwelt in the love of God and of man. Alike
    were they free from
Fear, that reigns with the tyrant, and envy, the
    vice of republics.
Neither locks had they to their doors, nor bars
    to their windows;
But their dwellings were open as day and the
    hearts of the owners;
There the richest was poor, and the poorest
    lived in abundance.
ℂ Somewhat apart from the village, and nearer
    the Basin of Minas,
Benedict Bellefontaine, the wealthiest farmer
    of Grand-Pré,
Dwelt on his goodly acres; and with him, di-
    recting his household,
Gentle Evangeline lived, his child, and the
    pride of the village.
Stalworth and stately in form was the man of
    seventy winters;
Hearty and hale was he, an oak that is covered
    with snow-flakes;

White as the snow were his locks, and his
    cheeks as brown as the oak-leaves.

Fair was she to behold, that maiden of seven-
    teen summers.

Black were her eyes as the berry that grows on
    the thorn by the wayside,

Black, yet how softly they gleamed beneath the
    brown shade of her tresses!

Sweet was her breath as the breath of kine
    that feed in the meadows.

When in the harvest heat she bore to the reap-
    ers at noontide

Flagons of home-brewed ale, ah! fair in sooth
    was the maiden.

Fairer was she when, on Sunday morn, while
    the bell from its turret

Sprinkled with holy sounds the air, as the priest
    with his hyssop

Sprinkles the congregation, and scatters bless-
    ings upon them,

Down the long street she passed, with her chap-
    let of beads and her missal,

Wearing her Norman cap, and her kirtle of
    blue, and the ear-rings,

Brought in the olden time from France, and
    since, as an heirloom,

Handed down from mother to child, through
    long generations.

But a celestial brightness—a more ethereal
    beauty—

Shone on her face and encircled her form,
    when, after confession,

Homeward serenely she walked with God's
    benediction upon her.

When she had passed, it seemed like the ceas-
    ing of exquisite music.

❡ Firmly builded with rafters of oak, the house
    of the farmer

Stood on the side of a hill commanding the
    sea; and a shady
Sycamore grew by the door, with a woodbine
    wreathing around it.
Rudely carved was the porch, with seats be-
    neath; and a footpath
Led through an orchard wide, and disappeared
    in the meadow.
Under the sycamore-tree were hives overhung
    by a penthouse,
Such as the traveller sees in regions remote by
    the roadside,
Built o'er a box for the poor, or the blessed
    image of Mary.
Farther down, on the slope of the hill, was the
    well with its moss-grown
Bucket, fastened with iron, and near it a trough
    for the horses.
Shielding the house from storms, on the north,
    were the barns and the farm-yard,
There stood the broad-wheeled wains and the
    antique ploughs and the harrows;
There were the folds for the sheep; and there,
    in his feathered seraglio,
Strutted the lordly turkey, and crowed the cock,
    with the selfsame
Voice that in ages of old had startled the peni-
    tent Peter.
Bursting with hay were the barns, themselves
    a village. In each one
Far o'er the gable projected a roof of thatch;
    and a staircase,
Under the sheltering eaves, led up to the odor-
    ous corn-loft.
There too the dove-cot stood, with its meek
    and innocent inmates
Murmuring ever of love; while above in the
    variant breezes

Numberless noisy weathercocks rattled and
    sang of mutation.

ℂ Thus, at peace with God and the world, the
    farmer of Grand-Pré

Lived on his sunny farm, and Evangeline gov-
    erned his household.

Many a youth, as he knelt in the church and
    opened his missal,

Fixed his eyes upon her, as the saint of his
    deepest devotion;

Happy was he who might touch her hand or
    the hem of her garment!

Many a suitor came to her door, by the dark-
    ness befriended,

And, as he knocked and waited to hear the
    sound of her footsteps,

Knew not which beat the louder, his heart or
    the knocker of iron;

Or at the joyous feast of the Patron Saint of
    the village,

Bolder grew, and pressed her hand in the dance
    as he whispered

Hurried words of love, that seemed a part of
    the music.

But, among all who came, young Gabriel only
    was welcome;

Gabriel Lajeunesse, the son of Basil the black-
    smith,

Who was a mighty man in the village, and
    honored of all men;

For, since the birth of time, throughout all ages
    and nations,

Has the craft of the smith been held in repute
    by the people.

Basil was Benedict's friend. Their children from
    earliest childhood

Grew up together as brother and sister; and
    Father Felician,

Priest and pedagogue both in the village, had
 taught them their letters
Out of the selfsame book, with the hymns of
 the church and the plain-song.
But when the hymn was sung, and the daily
 lesson completed,
Swiftly they hurried away to the forge of Basil'
 the blacksmith.
There at the door they stood, with wondering
 eyes to behold him
Take in his leathern lap the hoof of the horse
 as a plaything,
Nailing the shoe in its place; while near him
 the tire of the cart-wheel
Lay like a fiery snake, coiled round in a circle
 of cinders.
Oft on autumnal eves, when without in the
 gathering darkness
Bursting with light seemed the smithy, through
 every cranny and crevice,
Warm by the forge within they watched the
 laboring bellows,
And as its panting ceased, and the sparks ex-
 pired in the ashes,
Merrily laughed, and said they were nuns go-
 ing into the chapel.
Oft on sledges in winter, as swift as the swoop
 of the eagle,
Down the hillside bounding, they glided away
 o'er the meadow.
Oft in the barns they climbed to the populous
 nests on the rafters,
Seeking with eager eyes that wondrous stone,
 which the swallow
Brings from the shore of the sea to restore the
 sight of its fledglings;
Lucky was he who found that stone in the nest
 of the swallow!

Thus passed a few swift years, and they no
longer were children.

14 He was a valiant youth, and his face, like the
face of the morning,

Gladdened the earth with its light, and ripened
thought into action.

She was a woman now, with the heart and
hopes of a woman.

"Sunshine of Saint Eulalie" was she called;
for that was the sunshine

Which, as the farmers believed, would load
their orchards with apples;

She, too, would bring to her husband's house
delight and abundance,

Filling it full of love and the ruddy faces of
children.

≻ II ≺

Now had the season returned, when the nights grow colder and longer,
And the retreating sun the sign of the Scorpion enters.
Birds of passage sailed through the leaden air, from the ice-bound,
Desolate northern bays to the shores of tropical islands.
Harvests were gathered in; and wild with the winds of September
Wrestled the trees of the forest, as Jacob of old with the angel.
All the signs foretold a winter long and inclement.

Bees, with prophetic instinct of want, had
    hoarded their honey

Till the hives overflowed; and the Indian hunt-
    ers asserted

Cold would the winter be, for thick was the fur
    of the foxes.

Such was the advent of autumn. Then fol-
    lowed that beautiful season,

Called by the pious Acadian peasants the Sum-
    mer of All-Saints!

Filled was the air with a dreamy and magical
    light; and the landscape

Lay as if new-created in all the freshness of
    childhood.

Peace seemed to reign upon earth, and the rest-
    less heart of the ocean

Was for a moment consoled. All sounds were
    in harmony blended.

Voices of children at play, the crowing of cocks
    in the farm-yards,

Whir of wings in the drowsy air, and the coo-
    ing of pigeons,

All were subdued and low as the murmurs of
    love, and the great sun

Looked with the eye of love through the golden
    vapors around him;

While arrayed in its robes of russet and scarlet
    and yellow,

Bright with the sheen of the dew, each glit-
    tering tree of the forest

Flashed like the plane-tree the Persian adorned
    with mantles and jewels.

❦ Now recommenced the reign of rest and
    affection and stillness.

Day with its burden and heat had departed, and
    twilight descending

Brought back the evening star to the sky, and
    the herds to the homestead.

Pawing the ground they came, and resting their
    necks on each other,
And with their nostrils distended inhaling the
    freshness of evening.
Foremost, bearing the bell, Evangeline's beau-
    tiful heifer,
Proud of her snow-white hide, and the ribbon
    that waved from her collar,
Quietly paced and slow, as if conscious of
    human affection.
Then came the shepherd back with his bleating
    flocks from the seaside,
Where was their favorite pasture. Behind them
    followed the watch-dog,
Patient, full of importance, and grand in the
    pride of his instinct,
Walking from side to side with a lordly air,
    and superbly
Waving his bushy tail, and urging forward the
    stragglers;
Regent of flocks was he when the shepherd
    slept; their protector,
When from the forest at night, through the
    starry silence, the wolves howled.
Late, with the rising moon, returned the wains
    from the marshes,
Laden with briny hay, that filled the air with
    its odor.
Cheerily neighed the steeds, with dew on their
    manes and their fetlocks,
While aloft on their shoulders the wooden and
    ponderous saddles,
Painted with brilliant dyes, and adorned with
    tassels of crimson,
Nodded in bright array, like hollyhocks heavy
    with blossoms.
Patiently stood the cows meanwhile, and yield-
    ed their udders

Unto the milkmaid's hand; whilst loud and in
　　regular cadence
Into the sounding pails the foaming streamlets
　　descended.
Lowing of cattle and peals of laughter were
　　heard in the farm-yard,
Echoed back by the barns. Anon they sank into
　　stillness;
Heavily closed, with a jarring sound, the valves
　　of the barn-doors,
Rattled the wooden bars, and all for a season
　　was silent.
❡ In-doors, warm by the wide-mouthed fire-
　　place, idly the farmer
Sat in his elbow-chair, and watched how the
　　flames and the smoke-wreaths
Struggled together like foes in a burning city.
　　Behind him,
Nodding and mocking along the wall, with
　　gestures fantastic,
Darted his own huge shadow, and vanished
　　away into darkness.
Faces, clumsily carved in oak, on the back of
　　his arm-chair
Laughed in the flickering light, and the pewter
　　plates on the dresser
Caught and reflected the flame, as shields of
　　armies the sunshine.
Fragments of song the old man sang, and carols
　　of Christmas,
Such as at home, in the olden time, his fathers
　　before him
Sang in their Norman orchards and bright
　　Burgundian vineyards.
Close at her father's side was the gentle Evan-
　　geline seated,
Spinning flax for the loom, that stood in the
　　corner behind her.

Silent awhile were its treadles, at rest was its
diligent shuttle,
While the monotonous drone of the wheel, like
the drone of a bagpipe,
Followed the old man's song, and united the
fragments together.
As in a church, when the chant of the choir at
intervals ceases,
Footfalls are heard in the aisles, or words of
the priest at the altar,
So, in each pause of the song, with measured
motion the clock clicked.
❦ Thus as they sat, there were footsteps heard,
and, suddenly lifted,
Sounded the wooden latch, and the door swung
back on its hinges.
Benedict knew by the hob-nailed shoes it was
Basil the blacksmith,
And by her beating heart Evangeline knew
who was with him.
"Welcome!" the farmer exclaimed, as their
footsteps paused on the threshold,
"Welcome, Basil, my friend! Come, take thy
place on the settle
Close by the chimney-side, which is always
empty without thee;
Take from the shelf overhead thy pipe and the
box of tobacco;
Never so much thyself art thou as when through
the curling
Smoke of the pipe or the forge thy friendly and
jovial face gleams
Round and red as the harvest moon through
the mist of the marshes."
Then, with a smile of content, thus answered
Basil the blacksmith,
Taking with easy air the accustomed seat by
the fireside: —

"Benedict Bellefontaine, thou hast ever thy jest
    and thy ballad!
Ever in cheerfullest mood art thou, when others
    are filled with
Gloomy forebodings of ill, and see only ruin
    before them.
Happy art thou, as if every day thou hadst
    picked up a horseshoe."
Pausing a moment, to take the pipe that Evan-
    geline brought him,
And with a coal from the embers had lighted,
    he slowly continued: —
"Four days now are passed since the English
    ships at their anchors
Ride in the Gaspereau's mouth, with their can-
    non pointed against us.
What their design may be is unknown; but all
    are commanded
On the morrow to meet in the church, where
    his Majesty's mandate
Will be proclaimed as law in the land. Alas! in
    the mean time
Many surmises of evil alarm the hearts of the
    people."
Then made answer the farmer: — "Perhaps
    some friendlier purpose
Brings these ships to our shores. Perhaps the
    harvests in England
By untimely rains or untimelier heat have been
    blighted,
And from our bursting barns they would feed
    their cattle and children."
"Not so thinketh the folk in the village," said,
    warmly, the blacksmith,
Shaking his head, as in doubt; then, heaving a
    sigh, he continued —
"Louisburg is not forgotten, nor Beau Séjour,
    nor Port Royal.

Many already have fled to the forest, and lurk
    on its outskirts,
Waiting with anxious hearts the dubious fate
    of to-morrow.
Arms have been taken from us, and warlike
    weapons of all kinds;
Nothing is left but the blacksmith's sledge and
    the scythe of the mower."
Then with a pleasant smile made answer the
    jovial farmer : —
"Safer are we unarmed, in the midst of our
    flocks and our cornfields,
Safer within these peaceful dikes, besieged by
    the ocean,
Than our fathers in forts, besieged by the en-
    emy's cannon.
Fear no evil, my friend, and to-night may no
    shadow of sorrow
Fall on this house and hearth; for this is the
    night of the contract.
Built are the house and the barn. The merry
    lads of the village
Strongly have built them and well; and, break-
    ing the glebe round about them,
Filled the barn with hay, and the house with
    food for a twelvemonth.
René Leblanc will be here anon, with his papers
    and inkhorn.
Shall we not then be glad, and rejoice in the
    joy of our children?"
As apart by the window she stood, with her
    hand in her lover's,
Blushing Evangeline heard the words that her
    father had spoken,
And, as they died on his lips, the worthy notary
    entered.

➤ III ➤

Bᴇɴᴛ like a laboring oar, that toils in the surf
    of the ocean,
Bent, but not broken, by age was the form of
    the notary public;
Shocks of yellow hair, like the silken floss of
    the maize, hung
Over his shoulders; his forehead was high; and
    glasses with horn bows
Sat astride on his nose, with a look of wisdom
    supernal.
Father of twenty children was he, and more
    than a hundred
Children's children rode on his knee, and heard
    his great watch tick.

Four long years in the times of the war had he
    languished a captive,
Suffering much in an old French fort as the
    friend of the English.
Now, though warier grown, without all guile
    or suspicion,
Ripe in wisdom was he, but patient, and simple,
    and childlike.
He was beloved by all, and most of all by the
    children;
For he told them tales of the Loup-garou in the
    forest,
And of the goblin that came in the night to
    water the horses,
And of the white Létiche, the ghost of a child
    who unchristened
Died, and was doomed to haunt unseen the
    chambers of children;
And how on Christmas eve the oxen talked in
    the stable,
And how the fever was cured by a spider shut
    up in a nutshell,
And of the marvellous powers of four-leaved
    clover and horseshoes,
With whatsoever else was writ in the lore of the
    village.
Then up rose from his seat by the fireside Basil
    the blacksmith,
Knocked from his pipe the ashes, and slowly
    extending his right hand,
"Father Leblanc," he exclaimed, "thou hast
    heard the talk in the village,
And, perchance, canst tell us some news of
    these ships and their errand."
Then with modest demeanor made answer the
    notary public: —
"Gossip enough have I heard, in sooth, yet am
    never the wiser;

And what their errand may be I know not bet-
ter than others.

Yet am I not of those who imagine some evil
intention
Brings them here, for we are at peace; and why
then molest us?"
"God's name!" shouted the hasty and some-
what irascible blacksmith;
"Must we in all things look for the how, and
the why, and the wherefore?
Daily injustice is done, and might is the right
of the strongest!"
But, without heeding his warmth, continued
the notary public:—
"Man is unjust, but God is just; and finally
justice
Triumphs; and well I remember a story, that
often consoled me,
When as a captive I lay in the old French fort
at Port Royal."
This was the old man's favorite tale, and he
loved to repeat it
When his neighbors complained that any in-
justice was done them.
"Once in an ancient city, whose name I no
longer remember,
Raised aloft on a column, a brazen statue of
Justice
Stood in the public square, upholding the scales
in its left hand,
And in its right a sword, as an emblem that jus-
tice presided
Over the laws of the land, and the hearts and
homes of the people.
Even the birds had built their nests in the scales
of the balance,
Having no fear of the sword that flashed in the
sunshine above them.

But in the course of time the laws of the land
    were corrupted;
Might took the place of right, and the weak
    were oppressed, and the mighty
Ruled with an iron rod. Then it chanced in a
    nobleman's palace
That a necklace of pearls was lost, and erelong
    a suspicion
Fell on an orphan girl who lived as maid in the
    household.
She, after form of trial condemned to die on the
    scaffold,
Patiently met her doom at the foot of the statue
    of Justice.
As to her Father in heaven her innocent spirit
    ascended,
Lo! o'er the city a tempest rose; and the bolts
    of the thunder
Smote the statue of bronze, and hurled in wrath
    from its left hand
Down on the pavement below the clattering
    scales of the balance,
And in the hollow thereof was found the nest
    of a magpie,
Into whose clay-built walls the necklace of
    pearls was inwoven."
Silenced, but not convinced, when the story
    was ended, the blacksmith
Stood like a man who fain would speak, but
    findeth no language;
All his thoughts were congealed into lines on
    his face, as the vapors
Freeze in fantastic shapes on the window-panes
    in the winter.
❧ Then Evangeline lighted the brazen lamp on
    the table,
Filled, till it overflowed, the pewter tankard
    with home-brewed

Nut-brown ale, that was famed for its strength
in the village of Grand-Pré;

While from his pocket the notary drew his
papers and inkhorn,

Wrote with a steady hand the date and the age
of the parties,

Naming the dower of the bride in flocks of
sheep and in cattle.

Orderly all things proceeded, and duly and
well were completed,

And the great seal of the law was set like a
sun on the margin.

Then from his leathern pouch the farmer threw
on the table

Three times the old man's fee in solid pieces
of silver;

And the notary rising, and blessing the bride
and the bridegroom,

Lifted aloft the tankard of ale and drank to
their welfare.

Wiping the foam from his lip, he solemnly
bowed and departed,

While in silence the others sat and mused by
the fireside,

Till Evangeline brought the draught-board out
of its corner.

Soon was the game begun. In friendly conten-
tion the old men

Laughed at each lucky hit, or unsuccessful
manœuvre,

Laughed when a man was crowned, or a breach
was made in the king-row.

Meanwhile apart, in the twilight gloom of a
window's embrasure,

Sat the lovers, and whispered together, behold-
ing the moon rise

Over the pallid sea and the silvery mist of the
meadows.

Silently one by one, in the infinite meadows of
   heaven,
Blossomed the lovely stars, the forget-me-nots
   of the angels.
⁋ Thus was the evening passed. Anon the bell
   from the belfry
Rang out the hour of nine, the village curfew,
   and straightway
Rose the guests and departed; and silence
   reigned in the household.
Many a farewell word and sweet good night
   on the door-step
Lingered long in Evangeline's heart, and filled
   it with gladness.
Carefully then were covered the embers that
   glowed on the hearth-stone,
And on the oaken stairs resounded the tread
   of the farmer.
Soon with a soundless step the foot of Evange-
   line followed.
Up the staircase moved a luminous space in
   the darkness,
Lighted less by the lamp than the shining face
   of the maiden.
Silent she passed the hall, and entered the door
   of her chamber.
Simple that chamber was, with its curtains of
   white, and its clothes-press
Ample and high, on whose spacious shelves
   were carefully folded
Linen and woollen stuffs, by the hand of Evan-
   geline woven.
This was the precious dower she would bring
   to her husband in marriage,
Better than flocks and herds, being proofs of
   her skill as a housewife.
Soon she extinguished her lamp, for the mel-
   low and radiant moonlight

Streamed through the windows, and lighted
the room, till the heart of the maiden
Swelled and obeyed its power, like the tremu-
lous tides of the ocean.
Ah! she was fair, exceeding fair to behold, as
she stood with
Naked snow-white feet on the gleaming floor
of her chamber!
Little she dreamed that below, among the trees
of the orchard,
Waited her lover and watched for the gleam
of her lamp and her shadow.
Yet were her thoughts of him, and at times a
feeling of sadness
Passed o'er her soul, as the sailing shade of
clouds in the moonlight
Flitted across the floor and darkened the room
for a moment.
And, as she gazed from the window, she saw
serenely the moon pass
Forth from the folds of a cloud, and one star
follow her footsteps,
As out of Abraham's tent young Ishmael wan-
dered with Hagar!

≻ IV ≺

PLEASANTLY rose next morn the sun on the
    village of Grand-Pré.
Pleasantly gleamed in the soft, sweet air the
    Basin of Minas,
Where the ships, with their wavering shadows,
    were riding at anchor.
Life had long been astir in the village, and
    clamorous labor
Knocked with its hundred hands at the golden
    gates of the morning.
Now from the country around, from the farms
    and neighboring hamlets,
Came in their holiday dresses the blithe Aca-
    dian peasants.

Many a glad good morrow and jocund laugh
from the young folk
Made the bright air brighter, as up from the
numerous meadows,
Where no path could be seen but the track of
wheels in the greensward,
Group after group appeared, and joined, or
passed on the highway.
Long ere noon, in the village all sounds of labor
were silenced.
Thronged were the streets with people; and
noisy groups at the house-doors
Sat in the cheerful sun, and rejoiced and gos-
siped together.
Every house was an inn, where all were wel-
comed and feasted;
For with this simple people, who lived like
brothers together,
All things were held in common, and what one
had was another's.
Yet under Benedict's roof hospitality seemed
more abundant:
For Evangeline stood among the guests of her
father;
Bright was her face with smiles, and words of
welcome and gladness
Fell from her beautiful lips, and blessed the cup
as she gave it.
❡ Under the open sky, in the odorous air of the
orchard,
Stript of its golden fruit, was spread the feast of
betrothal.
There in the shade of the porch were the priest
and the notary seated;
There good Benedict sat, and sturdy Basil the
blacksmith.
Not far withdrawn from these, by the cider-
press and the beehives,

Michael the fiddler was placed, with the gayest
of hearts and of waistcoats.

Shadow and light from the leaves alternately
played on his snow-white

Hair, as it waved in the wind; and the jolly
face of the fiddler

Glowed like a living coal when the ashes are
blown from the embers.

Gayly the old man sang to the vibrant sound of
his fiddle,

Tous les Bourgeois de Chartres, and *Le Caril-
lon de Dunkerque,*

And anon with his wooden shoes beat time to
the music.

Merrily, merrily whirled the wheels of the diz-
zying dances

Under the orchard-trees and down the path to
the meadows;

Old folk and young together, and children
mingled among them.

Fairest of all the maids was Evangeline, Bene-
dict's daughter!

Noblest of all the youths was Gabriel, son of
the blacksmith!

❦ So passed the morning away. And lo! with a
summons sonorous

Sounded the bell from its tower, and over the
meadows a drum beat.

Thronged erelong was the church with men.
Without, in the churchyard,

Waited the women. They stood by the graves,
and hung on the headstones

Garlands of autumn-leaves and evergreens
fresh from the forest.

Then came the guard from the ships, and
marching proudly among them

Entered the sacred portal. With loud and dis-
sonant clangor

Echoed the sound of their brazen drums from
    ceiling and casement,—

Echoed a moment only, and slowly the pon-
    derous portal

Closed, and in silence the crowd awaited the
    will of the soldiers.

Then uprose their commander, and spake from
    the steps of the altar,

Holding aloft in his hands, with its seals, the
    royal commission.

"You are convened this day," he said, "by his
    Majesty's orders.

Clement and kind has he been; but how you
    have answered his kindness,

Let your own hearts reply! To my natural
    make and my temper

Painful the task is I do, which to you I know
    must be grievous.

Yet must I bow and obey, and deliver the will
    of our monarch;

Namely, that all your lands, and dwellings, and
    cattle of all kinds

Forfeited be to the crown; and that you your-
    selves from this province

Be transported to other lands. God grant you
    may dwell there

Ever as faithful subjects, a happy and peaceable
    people!

Prisoners now I declare you; for such is his
    Majesty's pleasure!"

As, when the air is serene in the sultry solstice
    of summer,

Suddenly gathers a storm, and the deadly sling
    of the hailstones

Beats down the farmer's corn in the field and
    shatters his windows,

Hiding the sun, and strewing the ground with
    thatch from the house-roofs,

Bellowing fly the herds, and seek to break their
    enclosures;

So on the hearts of the people descended the
    words of the speaker.

Silent a moment they stood in speechless won-
    der, and then rose

Louder and ever louder a wail of sorrow and
    anger,

And, by one impulse moved, they madly rushed
    to the door-way.

Vain was the hope of escape; and cries and
    fierce imprecations

Rang through the house of prayer; and high
    o'er the heads of the others

Rose, with his arms uplifted, the figure of Basil
    the blacksmith,

As, on a stormy sea, a spar is tossed by the
    billows.

Flushed was his face and distorted with pas-
    sion; and wildly he shouted, —

"Down with the tyrants of England! we never
    have sworn them allegiance!

Death to these foreign soldiers, who seize on
    our homes and our harvests!"

More he fain would have said, but the merci-
    less hand of a soldier

Smote him upon the mouth, and dragged him
    down to the pavement.

❦ In the midst of the strife and tumult of angry
    contention,

Lo! the door of the chancel opened, and Father
    Felician

Entered, with serious mien, and ascended the
    steps of the altar.

Raising his reverend hand, with a gesture he
    awed into silence

All that clamorous throng; and thus he spake
    to his people;

Deep were his tones and solemn; in accents
measured and mournful

Spake he, as, after the tocsin's alarum, distinctly
the clock strikes.

"What is this that ye do, my children? what
madness has seized you?

Forty years of my life have I labored among
you, and taught you,

Not in word alone, but in deed, to love one
another!

Is this the fruit of my toils, of my vigils and
prayers and privations?

Have you so soon forgotten all lessons of love
and forgiveness?

This is the house of the Prince of Peace, and
would you profane it

Thus with violent deeds and hearts overflow-
ing with hatred?

Lo! where the crucified Christ from his cross
is gazing upon you!

See! in those sorrowful eyes what meekness
and holy compassion!

Hark! how those lips still repeat the prayer,
'O Father, forgive them!'

Let us repeat that prayer in the hour when the
wicked assail us,

Let us repeat it now, and say, 'O Father, for-
give them!'"

Few were his words of rebuke, but deep in the
hearts of his people

Sank they, and sobs of contrition succeeded the
passionate outbreak,

While they repeated his prayer, and said, "O
Father, forgive them!"

❧ Then came the evening service. The tapers
gleamed from the altar.

Fervent and deep was the voice of the priest,
and the people responded,

Not with their lips alone, but their hearts; and
the Ave Maria

Sang they, and fell on their knees, and their
souls, with devotion translated,

Rose on the ardor of prayer, like Elijah ascend-
ing to heaven.

❡ Meanwhile had spread in the village the tid-
ings of ill, and on all sides

Wandered, wailing, from house to house the
women and children.

Long at her father's door Evangeline stood,
with her right hand

Shielding her eyes from the level rays of the
sun, that, descending,

Lighted the village street with mysterious splen-
dor, and roofed each

Peasant's cottage with golden thatch, and em-
blazoned its windows.

Long within had been spread the snow-white
cloth on the table;

There stood the wheaten loaf, and the honey
fragrant with wild-flowers;

There stood the tankard of ale, and the cheese
fresh brought from the dairy;

And, at the head of the board, the great arm-
chair of the farmer.

Thus did Evangeline wait at her father's door,
as the sunset

Threw the long shadows of trees o'er the broad
ambrosial meadows.

Ah! on her spirit within a deeper shadow had
fallen,

And from the fields of her soul a fragrance
celestial ascended, —

Charity, meekness, love, and hope, and forgive-
ness, and patience!

Then, all-forgetful of self, she wandered into
the village,

Cheering with looks and words the mournful
   hearts of the women,

As o'er the darkening fields with lingering steps
   they departed,

Urged by their household cares, and the weary
   feet of their children.

Down sank the great red sun, and in golden,
   glimmering vapors

Veiled the light of his face, like the Prophet
   descending from Sinai.

Sweetly over the village the bell of the Angelus
   sounded.

❦ Meanwhile, amid the gloom, by the church
   Evangeline lingered.

All was silent within; and in vain at the door
   and the windows

Stood she, and listened and looked, till, over-
   come by emotion,

"Gabriel!" cried she aloud with tremulous
   voice; but no answer

Came from the graves of the dead, nor the
   gloomier grave of the living.

Slowly at length she returned to the tenantless
   house of her father.

Smouldered the fire on the hearth, on the board
   was the supper untasted,

Empty and drear was each room, and haunted
   with phantoms of terror.

Sadly echoed her step on the stair and the floor
   of her chamber.

In the dead of the night she heard the discon-
   solate rain fall

Loud on the withered leaves of the sycamore-
   tree by the window.

Keenly the lightning flashed; and the voice of
   the echoing thunder

Told her that God was in heaven, and governed
   the world he created!

Then she remembered the tale she had heard of
    the justice of Heaven;
Soothed was her troubled soul, and she peace-   *37*
    fully slumbered till morning.

➤ V ➤

Four times the sun had risen and set; and now on the fifth day
Cheerily called the cock to the sleeping maids of the farm-house.
Soon o'er the yellow fields, in silent and mournful procession,
Came from the neighboring hamlets and farms the Acadian women,
Driving in ponderous wains their household goods to the sea-shore,
Pausing and looking back to gaze once more on their dwellings,
Ere they were shut from sight by the winding road and the woodland.

Close at their sides their children ran, and urged
on the oxen,
While in their little hands they clasped some
fragments of playthings.
ℭ Thus to the Gaspereau's mouth they hur-
ried; and there on the sea-beach
Piled in confusion lay the household goods of
the peasants.
All day long between the shore and the ships
did the boats ply;
All day long the wains came laboring down
from the village.
Late in the afternoon, when the sun was near
to his setting,
Echoed far o'er the fields came the rolls of
drums from the churchyard.
Thither the women and children thronged. On
a sudden the church-doors
Opened, and forth came the guard, and march-
ing in gloomy procession
Followed the long-imprisoned, but patient,
Acadian farmers.
Even as pilgrims, who journey afar from their
homes and their country,
Sing as they go, and in singing forget they are
weary and wayworn,
So with songs on their lips the Acadian peasants
descended
Down from the church to the shore, amid their
wives and their daughters.
Foremost the young men came; and, raising
together their voices,
Sang with tremulous lips a chant of the Catho-
lic Missions:—
"Sacred heart of the Saviour! O inexhaustible
fountain!
Fill our hearts this day with strength and sub-
mission and patience!"

Then the old men, as they marched, and the
women that stood by the wayside

Joined in the sacred psalm, and the birds in the
sunshine above them

Mingled their notes therewith, like voices of
spirits departed.

❡ Half-way down to the shore Evangeline
waited in silence,

Not overcome with grief, but strong in the
hour of affliction, —

Calmly and sadly she waited, until the proces-
sion approached her,

And she beheld the face of Gabriel pale with
emotion.

Tears then filled her eyes, and, eagerly running
to meet him,

Clasped she his hands, and laid her head on his
shoulder, and whispered, —

"Gabriel! be of good cheer! for if we love one
another,

Nothing, in truth, can harm us, whatever mis-
chances may happen!"

Smiling she spake these words; then suddenly
paused, for her father

Saw she slowly advancing. Alas! how changed
was his aspect!

Gone was the glow from his cheek, and the fire
from his eye, and his footstep

Heavier seemed with the weight of the heavy
heart in his bosom.

But with a smile and a sigh, she clasped his
neck and embraced him,

Speaking words of endearment where words of
comfort availed not.

Thus to the Gaspereau's mouth moved on that
mournful procession.

❡ There disorder prevailed, and the tumult and
stir of embarking.

Busily plied the freighted boats; and in the confusion
Wives were torn from their husbands, and mothers, too late, saw their children
Left on the land, extending their arms, with wildest entreaties.
So unto separate ships were Basil and Gabriel carried,
While in despair on the shore Evangeline stood with her father.
Half the task was not done when the sun went down, and the twilight
Deepened and darkened around; and in haste the refluent ocean
Fled away from the shore, and left the line of the sand-beach
Covered with waifs of the tide, with kelp and the slippery sea-weed.
Farther back in the midst of the household goods and the wagons,
Like to a gypsy camp, or a leaguer after a battle,
All escape cut off by the sea, and the sentinels near them,
Lay encamped for the night the houseless Acadian farmers.
Back to its nethermost caves retreated the bellowing ocean,
Dragging adown the beach the rattling pebbles, and leaving
Inland and far up the shore the stranded boats of the sailors.
Then, as the night descended, the herds returned from their pastures;
Sweet was the moist still air with the odor of milk from their udders;
Lowing they waited, and long, at the well-known bars of the farm-yard, —

Waited and looked in vain for the voice and the hand of the milkmaid.

Silence reigned in the streets; from the church no Angelus sounded,

Rose no smoke from the roofs, and gleamed no lights from the windows.

❡ But on the shores meanwhile the evening fires had been kindled,

Built of the drift-wood thrown on the sands from wrecks in the tempest.

Round them shapes of gloom and sorrowful faces were gathered,

Voices of women were heard, and of men, and the crying of children.

Onward from fire to fire, as from hearth to hearth in his parish,

Wandered the faithful priest, consoling and blessing and cheering,

Like unto shipwrecked Paul on Melita's desolate sea-shore.

Thus he approached the place where Evangeline sat with her father,

And in the flickering light beheld the face of the old man,

Haggard and hollow and wan, and without either thought or emotion,

E'en as the face of a clock from which the hands have been taken.

Vainly Evangeline strove with words and caresses to cheer him,

Vainly offered him food; yet he moved not, he looked not, he spake not,

But, with a vacant stare, ever gazed at the flickering fire-light.

"Benedicite!" murmured the priest, in tones of compassion.

More he fain would have said, but his heart was full, and his accents

Faltered and paused on his lips, as the feet of
    a child on a threshold,
Hushed by the scene he beholds, and the awful
    presence of sorrow.
Silently, therefore, he laid his hand on the head
    of the maiden,
Raising his tearful eyes to the silent stars that
    above them
Moved on their way, unperturbed by the
    wrongs and sorrows of mortals.
Then sat he down at her side, and they wept
    together in silence.
℃ Suddenly rose from the south a light, as in
    autumn the blood-red
Moon climbs the crystal walls of heaven, and
    o'er the horizon
Titan-like stretches its hundred hands upon
    mountain and meadow,
Seizing the rocks and the rivers, and piling
    huge shadows together.
Broader and ever broader it gleamed on the
    roofs of the village,
Gleamed on the sky and the sea, and the ships
    that lay in the roadstead.
Columns of shining smoke uprose, and flashes
    of flame were
Thrust through their folds and withdrawn,
    like the quivering hands of a martyr.
Then as the wind seized the gleeds and the
    burning thatch, and, uplifting,
Whirled them aloft through the air, at once
    from a hundred house-tops
Started the sheeted smoke with flashes of flame
    intermingled.
℃ These things beheld in dismay the crowd on
    the shore and on shipboard.
Speechless at first they stood, then cried aloud
    in their anguish,

"We shall behold no more our homes in the
  village of Grand-Pré!"

Loud on a sudden the cocks began to crow in
  the farm-yards,

Thinking the day had dawned; and anon the
  lowing of cattle

Came on the evening breeze, by the barking of
  dogs interrupted.

Then rose a sound of dread, such as startles the
  sleeping encampments

Far in the western prairies or forests that skirt
  the Nebraska,

When the wild horses affrighted sweep by with
  the speed of the whirlwind,

Or the loud bellowing herds of buffaloes rush
  to the river.

Such was the sound that arose on the night, as
  the herds and the horses

Broke through their folds and fences, and mad-
  ly rushed o'er the meadows.

℃ Overwhelmed with the sight, yet speechless,
  the priest and the maiden

Gazed on the scene of terror that reddened and
  widened before them;

And as they turned at length to speak to their
  silent companion,

Lo! from his seat he had fallen, and stretched
  abroad on the sea-shore

Motionless lay his form, from which the soul
  had departed.

Slowly the priest uplifted the lifeless head, and
  the maiden

Knelt at her father's side, and wailed aloud in
  her terror.

Then in a swoon she sank, and lay with her
  head on his bosom.

Through the long night she lay in deep, ob-
  livious slumber;

And when she woke from the trance, she beheld a multitude near her.

Faces of friends she beheld, that were mournfully gazing upon her,

Pallid, with tearful eyes, and looks of saddest compassion.

Still the blaze of the burning village illumined the landscape,

Reddened the sky overhead, and gleamed on the faces around her,

And like the day of doom it seemed to her wavering senses.

Then a familiar voice she heard, as it said to the people, —

"Let us bury him here by the sea. When a happier season

Brings us again to our homes from the unknown land of our exile,

Then shall his sacred dust be piously laid in the churchyard."

Such were the words of the priest. And there in haste by the seaside,

Having the glare of the burning village for funeral torches,

But without bell or book, they buried the farmer of Grand-Pré.

And as the voice of the priest repeated the service of sorrow,

Lo! with a mournful sound, like the voice of a vast congregation,

Solemnly answered the sea, and mingled its roar with the dirges.

'Twas the returning tide, that afar from the waste of the ocean,

With the first dawn of the day, came heaving and hurrying landward.

Then recommenced once more the stir and noise of embarking;

And with the ebb of the tide the ships sailed
    out of the harbor,

46 Leaving behind them the dead on the shore,
    and the village in ruins.

PART THE SECOND

⊱ I ⊰

MANY a weary year had passed since the
burning of Grand-Pré,
When on the falling tide the freighted vessels
departed,
Bearing a nation, with all its household gods,
into exile,
Exile without an end, and without an example
in story.
Far asunder, on separate coasts, the Acadians
landed;
Scattered were they, like flakes of snow, when
the wind from the northeast

Strikes aslant through the fogs that darken the
Banks of Newfoundland.

Friendless, homeless, hopeless, they wandered
from city to city,

From the cold lakes of the North to sultry
Southern savannas, —

From the bleak shores of the sea to the lands
where the Father of Waters

Seizes the hills in his hands, and drags them
down to the ocean,

Deep in their sands to bury the scattered bones
of the mammoth.

Friends they sought and homes; and many,
despairing, heart-broken,

Asked of the earth but a grave, and no longer
a friend nor a fireside.

Written their history stands on tablets of stone
in the churchyards.

℃ Long among them was seen a maiden who
waited and wandered,

Lowly and meek in spirit, and patiently suffer-
ing all things.

Fair was she and young; but, alas! before her
extended,

Dreary and vast and silent, the desert of life,
with its pathway

Marked by the graves of those who had sor-
rowed and suffered before her,

Passions long extinguished, and hopes long
dead and abandoned,

As the emigrant's way o'er the Western desert
is marked by

Camp-fires long consumed, and bones that
bleach in the sunshine.

Something there was in her life incomplete,
imperfect, unfinished;

As if a morning of June, with all its music and
sunshine,

Suddenly paused in the sky, and, fading, slow-
ly descended

Into the east again, from whence it late had
arisen.

Sometimes she lingered in towns, till, urged by
the fever within her,

Urged by a restless longing, the hunger and
thirst of the spirit,

She would commence again her endless search
and endeavor;

Sometimes in churchyards strayed, and gazed
on the crosses and tombstones,

Sat by some nameless grave, and thought that
perhaps in its bosom

He was already at rest, and she longed to slum-
ber beside him.

Sometimes a rumor, a hearsay, an inarticulate
whisper,

Came with its airy hand to point and beckon
her forward.

Sometimes she spake with those who had seen
her beloved and known him,

But it was long ago, in some far-off place or
forgotten.

"Gabriel Lajeunesse!" they said; "O yes! we
have seen him.

He was with Basil the blacksmith, and both
have gone to the prairies;

Coureurs-des-Bois are they, and famous hunters
and trappers."

"Gabriel Lajeunesse!" said others; "O yes! we
have seen him.

He is a Voyageur in the lowlands of Louisi-
ana."

Then would they say, "Dear child! why dream
and wait for him longer?

Are there not other youths as fair as Gabriel?
others

Who have hearts as tender and true, and spirits
    as loyal?

Here is Baptiste Leblanc, the notary's son, who
    has loved thee

Many a tedious year; come, give him thy hand
    and be happy!

Thou art too fair to be left to braid St. Cather-
    ine's tresses."

Then would Evangeline answer, serenely but
    sadly, "I cannot!

Whither my heart has gone, there follows my
    hand, and not elsewhere.

For when the heart goes before, like a lamp,
    and illumines the pathway,

Many things are made clear, that else lie hid-
    den in darkness."

Thereupon the priest, her friend and father-
    confessor,

Said, with a smile, "O daughter! thy God thus
    speaketh within thee!

Talk not of wasted affection, affection never
    was wasted;

If it enrich not the heart of another, its waters,
    returning

Back to their springs, like the rain, shall fill
    them full of refreshment;

That which the fountain sends forth returns
    again to the fountain.

Patience; accomplish thy labor; accomplish thy
    work of affection!

Sorrow and silence are strong, and patient en-
    durance is godlike.

Therefore accomplish thy labor of love, till the
    heart is made godlike,

Purified, strengthened, perfected, and rendered
    more worthy of heaven!"

Cheered by the good man's words, Evangeline
    labored and waited.

Still in her heart she heard the funeral dirge of
the ocean,
But with its sound there was mingled a voice
that whispered, "Despair not!"
Thus did that poor soul wander in want and
cheerless discomfort,
Bleeding, barefooted, over the shards and thorns
of existence.
Let me essay, O Muse! to follow the wander-
er's footsteps; —
Not through each devious path, each changeful
year of existence;
But as a traveller follows a streamlet's course
through the valley:
Far from its margin at times, and seeing the
gleam of its water
Here and there, in some open space, and at
intervals only;
Then drawing nearer its banks, through sylvan
glooms that conceal it,
Though he behold it not, he can hear its con-
tinuous murmur;
Happy, at length, if he find the spot where it
reaches an outlet.

➤ II ◄

I⊤ was the month of May. Far down the Beau-
  tiful River,
Past the Ohio shore and past the mouth of the
  Wabash,
Into the golden stream of the broad and swift
  Mississippi,
Floated a cumbrous boat, that was rowed by
  Acadian boatmen.
It was a band of exiles: a raft, as it were, from
  the shipwrecked
Nation, scattered along the coast, now floating
  together,
Bound by the bonds of a common belief and a
  common misfortune;

Men and women and children, who, guided by
     hope or by hearsay,
Sought for their kith and their kin among the
     few-acred farmers
On the Acadian coast, and the prairies of fair
     Opelousas.
With them Evangeline went, and her guide,
     the Father Felician.
Onward o'er sunken sands, through a wilder-
     ness sombre with forests,
Day after day they glided adown the turbulent
     river;
Night after night, by their blazing fires, en-
     camped on its borders.
Now through rushing chutes, among green
     islands, where plumelike
Cotton-trees nodded their shadowy crests, they
     swept with the current,
Then emerged into broad lagoons, where sil-
     very sand-bars
Lay in the stream, and along the wimpling
     waves of their margin,
Shining with snow-white plumes, large flocks
     of pelicans waded.
Level the landscape grew, and along the shores
     of the river,
Shaded by china-trees, in the midst of luxuriant
     gardens,
Stood the houses of planters, with negro-cabins
     and dove-cots.
They were approaching the region where reigns
     perpetual summer,
Where through the Golden Coast, and groves
     of orange and citron,
Sweeps with majestic curve the river away to
     the eastward.
They, too, swerved from their course; and,
     entering the Bayou of Plaquemine,

Soon were lost in a maze of sluggish and devious waters,

Which, like a network of steel, extended in every direction.

Over their heads the towering and tenebrous boughs of the cypress

Met in a dusky arch, and trailing mosses in mid-air

Waved like banners that hang on the walls of ancient cathedrals.

Deathlike the silence seemed, and unbroken, save by the herons

Home to their roosts in the cedar-trees returning at sunset,

Or by the owl, as he greeted the moon with demoniac laughter.

Lovely the moonlight was as it glanced and gleamed on the water,

Gleamed on the columns of cypress and cedar sustaining the arches,

Down through whose broken vaults it fell as through chinks in a ruin.

Dreamlike, and indistinct, and strange were all things around them;

And o'er their spirits there came a feeling of wonder and sadness, —

Strange forebodings of ill, unseen and that cannot be compassed.

As, at the tramp of a horse's hoof on the turf of the prairies,

Far in advance are closed the leaves of the shrinking mimosa,

So, at the hoof-beats of fate, with sad forebodings of evil,

Shrinks and closes the heart, ere the stroke of doom has attained it.

But Evangeline's heart was sustained by a vision, that faintly

Floated before her eyes, and beckoned her on
through the moonlight.

It was the thought of her brain that assumed
the shape of a phantom.

Through those shadowy aisles had Gabriel
wandered before her,

And every stroke of the oar now brought him
nearer and nearer.

❦ Then in his place, at the prow of the boat,
rose one of the oarsmen,

And, as a signal sound, if others like them per-
adventure

Sailed on those gloomy and midnight streams,
blew a blast on his bugle.

Wild through the dark colonnades and corri-
dors leafy the blast rang,

Breaking the seal of silence, and giving tongues
to the forest.

Soundless above them the banners of moss just
stirred to the music.

Multitudinous echoes awoke and died in the
distance,

Over the watery floor, and beneath the rever-
berant branches;

But not a voice replied; no answer came from
the darkness;

And, when the echoes had ceased, like a sense
of pain was the silence.

Then Evangeline slept; but the boatmen rowed
through the midnight,

Silent at times, then singing familiar Canadian
boat-songs,

Such as they sang of old on their own Acadian
rivers,

While through the night were heard the mys-
terious sounds of the desert,

Far off,—indistinct,—as of wave or wind in
the forest,

Mixed with the whoop of the crane and the
    roar of the grim alligator.

❡ Thus ere another noon they emerged from
    the shades; and before them

Lay, in the golden sun, the lakes of the Atcha-
    falaya.

Water-lilies in myriads rocked on the slight
    undulations

Made by the passing oars, and, resplendent in
    beauty, the lotus

Lifted her golden crown above the heads of the
    boatmen.

Faint was the air with the odorous breath of
    magnolia blossoms,

And with the heat of noon; and numberless
    sylvan islands,

Fragrant and thickly embowered with blos-
    soming hedges of roses,

Near to whose shores they glided along, invited
    to slumber.

Soon by the fairest of these their weary oars
    were suspended.

Under the boughs of Wachita willows, that
    grew by the margin,

Safely their boat was moored; and scattered
    about on the greensward,

Tired with their midnight toil, the weary trav-
    ellers slumbered.

Over them vast and high extended the cope of
    a cedar.

Swinging from its great arms, the trumpet-
    flower and the grape-vine

Hung their ladder of ropes aloft like the ladder
    of Jacob,

On whose pendulous stairs the angels ascend-
    ing, descending,

Were the swift humming-birds, that flitted
    from blossom to blossom.

Such was the vision Evangeline saw as she
    slumbered beneath it.
Filled was her heart with love, and the dawn of an opening heaven
Lighted her soul in sleep with the glory of
    regions celestial.
❦ Nearer and ever nearer, among the number-
    less islands,
Darted a light, swift boat, that sped away o'er
    the water,
Urged on its course by the sinewy arms of hunt-
    ers and trappers.
Northward its prow was turned, to the land of
    the bison and beaver.
At the helm sat a youth, with countenance
    thoughtful and care-worn.
Dark and neglected locks overshadowed his
    brow, and a sadness
Somewhat beyond his years on his face was
    legibly written.
Gabriel was it, who, weary with waiting, un-
    happy and restless,
Sought in the Western wilds oblivion of self
    and of sorrow.
Swiftly they glided along, close under the lee of
    the island,
But by the opposite bank, and behind a screen
    of palmettos,
So that they saw not the boat, where it lay con-
    cealed in the willows,
All undisturbed by the dash of their oars, and
    unseen, were the sleepers,
Angel of God was there none to awaken the
    slumbering maiden.
Swiftly they glided away, like the shade of a
    cloud on the prairie.
After the sound of their oars on the tholes had
    died in the distance,

57

As from a magic trance the sleepers awoke,
and the maiden

Said with a sigh to the friendly priest, "O Father
Felician!

Something says in my heart that near me
Gabriel wanders.

Is it a foolish dream, an idle and vague super-
stition?

Or has an angel passed, and revealed the truth
to my spirit?"

Then, with a blush, she added, "Alas for my
credulous fancy!

Unto ears like thine such words as these have
no meaning."

But made answer the reverend man, and he
smiled as he answered, —

"Daughter, thy words are not idle; nor are they
to me without meaning.

Feeling is deep and still; and the word that
floats on the surface

Is as the tossing buoy, that betrays where the
anchor is hidden.

Therefore trust to thy heart, and to what the
world calls illusions.

Gabriel truly is near thee; for not far away to
the southward,

On the banks of the Têche, are the towns of St.
Maur and St. Martin.

There the long-wandering bride shall be given
again to her bridegroom,

There the long-absent pastor regain his flock
and his sheepfold.

Beautiful is the land, with its prairies and for-
ests of fruit-trees;

Under the feet a garden of flowers, and the
bluest of heavens

Bending above, and resting its dome on the
walls of the forest.

They who dwell there have named it the Eden
    of Louisiana."

❦ With these words of cheer they arose and
    continued their journey.

Softly the evening came. The sun from the
    western horizon

Like a magician extended his golden wand o'er
    the landscape;

Twinkling vapors arose; and sky and water
    and forest

Seemed all on fire at the touch, and melted and
    mingled together.

Hanging between two skies, a cloud with edges
    of silver,

Floated the boat, with its dripping oars, on the
    motionless water.

Filled was Evangeline's heart with inexpress-
    ible sweetness.

Touched by the magic spell, the sacred foun-
    tains of feeling

Glowed with the light of love, as the skies and
    waters around her.

Then from a neighboring thicket the mocking-
    bird, wildest of singers,

Swinging aloft on a willow spray that hung
    o'er the water,

Shook from his little throat such floods of de-
    lirious music,

That the whole air and the woods and the
    waves seemed silent to listen.

Plaintive at first were the tones and sad; then
    soaring to madness

Seemed they to follow or guide the revel of
    frenzied Bacchantes.

Single notes were then heard, in sorrowful, low
    lamentation;

Till, having gathered them all, he flung them
    abroad in derision,

As when, after a storm, a gust of wind through
the tree-tops

Shakes down the rattling rain in a crystal show-
er on the branches.

With such a prelude as this, and hearts that
throbbed with emotion,

Slowly they entered the Têche, where it flows
through the green Opelousas,

And, through the amber air, above the crest of
the woodland,

Saw the column of smoke that arose from a
neighboring dwelling; —

Sounds of a horn they heard, and the distant
lowing of cattle.

⊱ III ⊰

Near to the bank of the river, o'ershadowed
  by oaks, from whose branches
Garlands of Spanish moss and of mystic mistle-
  toe flaunted,
Such as the Druids cut down with golden
  hatchets at Yule-tide,
Stood, secluded and still, the house of the herds-
  man. A garden
Girded it round about with a belt of luxuriant
  blossoms,
Filling the air with fragrance. The house itself
  was of timbers
Hewn from the cypress-tree, and carefully fit-
  ted together.

Large and low was the roof; and on slender
columns supported,
Rose-wreathed, vine-encircled, a broad and spa-
cious veranda,
Haunt of the humming-bird and the bee, ex-
tended around it.
At each end of the house, amid the flowers of
the garden,
Stationed the dove-cots were, as love's perpetual
symbol,
Scenes of endless wooing, and endless conten-
tions of rivals.
Silence reigned o'er the place. The line of
shadow and sunshine
Ran near the tops of the trees; but the house
itself was in shadow,
And from its chimney-top, ascending and slow-
ly expanding
Into the evening air, a thin blue column of
smoke rose.
In the rear of the house, from the garden gate,
ran a pathway
Through the great groves of oak to the skirts
of the limitless prairie,
Into whose sea of flowers the sun was slowly
descending.
Full in his track of light, like ships with shad-
owy canvas
Hanging loose from their spars in a motionless
calm in the tropics,
Stood a cluster of trees, with tangled cordage
of grape-vines.
❡ Just where the woodlands met the flowery
surf of the prairie,
Mounted upon his horse, with Spanish saddle
and stirrups,
Sat a herdsman, arrayed in gaiters and doublet
of deerskin.

Broad and brown was the face that from under
the Spanish sombrero

Gazed on the peaceful scene, with the lordly
look of its master.

Round about him were numberless herds of
kine, that were grazing

Quietly in the meadows, and breathing the
vapory freshness

That uprose from the river, and spread itself
over the landscape.

Slowly lifting the horn that hung at his side,
and expanding

Fully his broad, deep chest, he blew a blast,
that resounded

Wildly and sweet and far, through the still
damp air of the evening.

Suddenly out of the grass the long white horns
of the cattle

Rose like flakes of foam on the adverse currents
of ocean.

Silent a moment they gazed, then bellowing
rushed o'er the prairie,

And the whole mass became a cloud, a shade in
the distance.

Then, as the herdsman turned to the house,
through the gate of the garden

Saw he the forms of the priest and the maiden
advancing to meet him.

Suddenly down from his horse he sprang in
amazement, and forward

Rushed with extended arms and exclamations
of wonder;

When they beheld his face, they recognized
Basil the blacksmith.

Hearty his welcome was, as he led his guests to
the garden.

There in an arbor of roses with endless ques-
tion and answer

Gave they vent to their hearts, and renewed their friendly embraces,

Laughing and weeping by turns, or sitting silent and thoughtful.

Thoughtful, for Gabriel came not; and now dark doubts and misgivings

Stole o'er the maiden's heart; and Basil, somewhat embarrassed,

Broke the silence and said, "If you came by the Atchafalaya,

How have you nowhere encountered my Gabriel's boat on the bayous?"

Over Evangeline's face at the words of Basil a shade passed.

Tears came into her eyes, and she said, with a tremulous accent,

"Gone? is Gabriel gone?" and, concealing her face on his shoulder,

All her o'erburdened heart gave way, and she wept and lamented.

Then the good Basil said, — and his voice grew blithe as he said it, —

"Be of good cheer, my child; it is only to-day he departed.

Foolish boy! he has left me alone with my herds and my horses.

Moody and restless grown, and tried and troubled, his spirit

Could no longer endure the calm of this quiet existence.

Thinking ever of thee, uncertain and sorrowful ever,

Ever silent, or speaking only of thee and his troubles,

He at length had become so tedious to men and to maidens,

Tedious even to me, that at length I bethought me, and sent him

Unto the town of Adayes to trade for mules
  with the Spaniards.

Thence he will follow the Indian trails to the
  Ozark Mountains,

Hunting for furs in the forests, on rivers trap-
  ping the beaver.

Therefore be of good cheer; we will follow the
  fugitive lover;

He is not far on his way, and the Fates and the
  streams are against him.

Up and away to-morrow, and through the red
  dew of the morning

We will follow him fast, and bring him back
  to his prison."

⊄ Then glad voices were heard, and up from
  the banks of the river,

Borne aloft on his comrades' arms, came Mi-
  chael the fiddler.

Long under Basil's roof had he lived like a god
  on Olympus,

Having no other care than dispensing music to
  mortals.

Far renowned was he for his silver locks and
  his fiddle.

"Long live Michael," they cried, "our brave
  Acadian minstrel!"

As they bore him aloft in triumphal procession;
  and straightway

Father Felician advanced with Evangeline,
  greeting the old man

Kindly and oft, and recalling the past, while
  Basil, enraptured,

Hailed with hilarious joy his old companions
  and gossips,

Laughing loud and long, and embracing moth-
  ers and daughters.

Much they marvelled to see the wealth of the
  ci-devant blacksmith,

All his domains and his herds, and his patri-
    archal demeanor;

Much they marvelled to hear his tales of the
    soil and the climate,

And of the prairies, whose numberless herds
    were his who would take them;

Each one thought in his heart, that he, too,
    would go and do likewise.

Thus they ascended the steps, and, crossing the
    breezy veranda,

Entered the hall of the house, where already
    the supper of Basil

Waited his late return; and they rested and
    feasted together.

℃ Over the joyous feast the sudden darkness
    descended.

All was silent without, and, illuming the land-
    scape with silver,

Fair rose the dewy moon and the myriad stars;
    but within doors,

Brighter than these, shone the faces of friends
    in the glimmering lamplight.

Then from his station aloft, at the head of the
    table, the herdsman

Poured forth his heart and his wine together
    in endless profusion.

Lighting his pipe, that was filled with sweet
    Natchitoches tobacco,

Thus he spake to his guests, who listened, and
    smiled as they listened: —

"Welcome once more, my friends, who long
    have been friendless and homeless,

Welcome once more to a home, that is better
    perchance than the old one!

Here no hungry winter congeals our blood like
    the rivers;

Here no stony ground provokes the wrath of
    the farmer.

Smoothly the ploughshare runs through the
    soil, as a keel through the water.
All the year round the orange-groves are in
    blossom; and grass grows
More in a single night than a whole Canadian
    summer.
Here, too, numberless herds run wild and un-
    claimed in the prairies;
Here, too, lands may be had for the asking, and
    forests of timber
With a few blows of the axe are hewn and
    framed into houses.
After your houses are built, and your fields are
    yellow with harvests,
No King George of England shall drive you
    away from your homesteads,
Burning your dwellings and barns, and steal-
    ing your farms and your cattle."
Speaking these words, he blew a wrathful cloud
    from his nostrils,
While his huge, brown hand came thundering
    down on the table,
So that the guests all started; and Father Fe-
    lician, astounded,
Suddenly paused, with a pinch of snuff half-
    way to his nostrils.
But the brave Basil resumed, and his words
    were milder and gayer:—
"Only beware of the fever, my friends, beware
    of the fever!
For it is not like that of our cold Acadian
    climate,
Cured by wearing a spider hung round one's
    neck in a nutshell!"
Then there were voices heard at the door, and
    footsteps approaching
Sounded upon the stairs and the floor of the
    breezy veranda.

It was the neighboring Creoles and small Acadian planters,

Who had been summoned all to the house of
Basil the Herdsman.

Merry the meeting was of ancient comrades
and neighbors:

Friend clasped friend in his arms; and they
who before were as strangers,

Meeting in exile, became straightway as friends
to each other,

Drawn by the gentle bond of a common country together.

But in the neighboring hall a strain of music,
proceeding

From the accordant strings of Michael's melodious fiddle,

Broke up all further speech. Away, like children delighted,

All things forgotten beside, they gave themselves to the maddening

Whirl of the dizzy dance, as it swept and swayed to the music,

Dreamlike, with beaming eyes and the rush of
fluttering garments.

❦ Meanwhile, apart, at the head of the hall, the
priest and the herdsman

Sat, conversing together of past and present
and future;

While Evangeline stood like one entranced, for
within her

Olden memories rose, and loud in the midst of
the music

Heard she the sound of the sea, and an irrepressible sadness

Came o'er her heart, and unseen she stole forth
into the garden.

Beautiful was the night. Behind the black wall
of the forest,

Tipping its summit with silver, arose the moon. On the river
Fell here and there through the branches a tremulous gleam of the moonlight,
Like the sweet thoughts of love on a darkened and devious spirit.
Nearer and round about her, the manifold flowers of the garden
Poured out their souls in odors, that were their prayers and confessions
Unto the night, as it went its way like a silent Carthusian.
Fuller of fragrance than they, and as heavy with shadows and night-dews,
Hung the heart of the maiden. The calm and the magical moonlight
Seemed to inundate her soul with indefinable longings,
As, through the garden gate, and beneath the shade of the oak-trees,
Passed she along the path to the edge of the measureless prairie.
Silent it lay, with a silvery haze upon it, and fireflies
Gleaming and floating away in mingled and infinite numbers.
Over her head the stars, the thoughts of God in the heavens,
Shone on the eyes of man, who had ceased to marvel and worship,
Save when a blazing comet was seen on the walls of that temple,
As if a hand had appeared and written upon them, "Upharsin."
And the soul of the maiden, between the stars and the fireflies,
Wandered alone, and she cried, "O Gabriel! O my beloved!

Art thou so near unto me, and yet I cannot
    behold thee?

Art thou so near unto me, and yet thy voice
    does not reach me?

Ah! how often thy feet have trod this path to
    the prairie!

Ah! how often thine eyes have looked on the
    woodlands around me!

Ah! how often beneath this oak, returning
    from labor,

Thou hast lain down to rest, and to dream of
    me in thy slumbers.

When shall these eyes behold, these arms be
    folded about thee?"

Loud and sudden and near the note of a whip-
    poorwill sounded

Like a flute in the woods; and anon, through
    the neighboring thickets,

Farther and farther away it floated and dropped
    into silence.

"Patience!" whispered the oaks from oracular
    caverns of darkness;

And, from the moonlit meadow, a sigh re-
    sponded, "To-morrow!"

❦ Bright rose the sun next day; and all the
    flowers of the garden

Bathed his shining feet with their tears, and
    anointed his tresses

With the delicious balm that they bore in their
    vases of crystal.

"Farewell!" said the priest, as he stood at the
    shadowy threshold;

"See that you bring us the Prodigal Son from
    his fasting and famine,

And, too, the Foolish Virgin, who slept when
    the bridegroom was coming."

"Farewell!" answered the maiden, and, smil-
    ing, with Basil descended

Down to the river's brink, where the boatmen
    already were waiting.
Thus beginning their journey with morning,
    and sunshine, and gladness,
Swiftly they followed the flight of him who
    was speeding before them,
Blown by the blast of fate like a dead leaf over
    the desert.
Not that day, nor the next, nor yet the day that
    succeeded,
Found they trace of his course, in lake or forest
    or river,
Nor, after many days, had they found him; but
    vague and uncertain
Rumors alone were their guides through a wild
    and desolate country;
Till, at the little inn of the Spanish town of
    Adayes,
Weary and worn, they alighted, and learned
    from the garrulous landlord,
That on the day before, with horses and guides
    and companions,
Gabriel left the village, and took the road of
    the prairies.

⊰ IV ⊱

Far in the West there lies a desert land, where
the mountains
Lift, through perpetual snows, their lofty and
luminous summits.
Down from their jagged, deep ravines, where
the gorge, like a gateway,
Opens a passage rude to the wheels of the emi-
grant's wagon,
Westward the Oregon flows and the Walleway
and Owyhee.
Eastward, with devious course, among the
Wind-river Mountains,
Through the Sweet-water Valley precipitate
leaps the Nebraska;

And to the south, from Fontaine-qui-bout and
　　the Spanish sierras,
Fretted with sands and rocks, and swept by
　　the wind of the desert,
Numberless torrents, with ceaseless sound, de-
　　scend to the ocean,
Like the great chords of a harp, in loud and
　　solemn vibrations.
Spreading between these streams are the won-
　　drous, beautiful prairies,
Billowy bays of grass ever rolling in shadow
　　and sunshine,
Bright with luxuriant clusters of roses and
　　purple amorphas.
Over them wandered the buffalo herds, and the
　　elk and the roebuck;
Over them wandered the wolves, and herds of
　　riderless horses;
Fires that blast and blight, and winds that are
　　weary with travel;
Over them wander the scattered tribes of Ish-
　　mael's children,
Staining the desert with blood; and above their
　　terrible war-trails
Circles and sails aloft, on pinions majestic, the
　　vulture,
Like the implacable soul of a chieftain slaugh-
　　tered in battle,
By invisible stairs ascending and scaling the
　　heavens.
Here and there rise smokes from the camps of
　　these savage marauders;
Here and there rise groves from the margins
　　of swift-running rivers;
And the grim, taciturn bear, the anchorite
　　monk of the desert,
Climbs down their dark ravines to dig for roots
　　by the brookside,

And over all is the sky, the clear and crystalline heaven,

Like the protecting hand of God inverted above them.

℃ Into this wonderful land, at the base of the Ozark Mountains,

Gabriel far had entered, with hunters and trappers behind him.

Day after day, with their Indian guides, the maiden and Basil

Followed his flying steps, and thought each day to o'ertake him.

Sometimes they saw, or thought they saw, the smoke of his camp-fire

Rise in the morning air from the distant plain; but at nightfall,

When they had reached the place, they found only embers and ashes.

And, though their hearts were sad at times and their bodies were weary,

Hope still guided them on, as the magic Fata Morgana

Showed them her lakes of light, that retreated and vanished before them.

℃ Once, as they sat by their evening fire, there silently entered

Into the little camp an Indian woman, whose features

Wore deep traces of sorrow, and patience as great as her sorrow.

She was a Shawnee woman returning home to her people,

From the far-off hunting-grounds of the cruel Camanches,

Where her Canadien husband, a Coureur-des-Bois, had been murdered.

Touched were their hearts at her story, and warmest and friendliest welcome

Gave they, with words of cheer, and she sat and
    feasted among them
On the buffalo-meat and the venison cooked on
    the embers.
But when their meal was done, and Basil and
    all his companions,
Worn with the long day's march and the chase
    of the deer and the bison,
Stretched themselves on the ground, and slept
    where the quivering fire-light
Flashed on their swarthy cheeks, and their
    forms wrapped up in their blankets,
Then at the door of Evangeline's tent she sat
    and repeated
Slowly, with soft, low voice, and the charm of
    her Indian accent,
All the tale of her love, with its pleasures, and
    pains, and reverses.
Much Evangeline wept at the tale, and to know
    that another
Hapless heart like her own had loved and had
    been disappointed.
Moved to the depths of her soul by pity and
    woman's compassion,
Yet in her sorrow pleased that one who had
    suffered was near her,
She in turn related her love and all its disas-
    ters.
Mute with wonder the Shawnee sat, and when
    she had ended
Still was mute; but at length, as if a mysterious
    horror
Passed through her brain, she spake, and re-
    peated the tale of the Mowis;
Mowis, the bridegroom of snow, who won and
    wedded a maiden,
But, when the morning came, arose and passed
    from the wigwam,

Fading and melting away and dissolving into
the sunshine,

Till she beheld him no more, though she fol-
lowed far into the forest.

Then, in those sweet, low tones, that seemed
like a weird incantation,

Told she the tale of the fair Lilinau, who was
wooed by a phantom,

That, through the pines o'er her father's lodge,
in the hush of the twilight,

Breathed like the evening wind, and whispered
love to the maiden,

Till she followed his green and waving plume
through the forest,

And never more returned, nor was seen again
by her people.

Silent with wonder and strange surprise, Evan-
geline listened

To the soft flow of her magical words, till the
region around her

Seemed like enchanted ground, and her swar-
thy guest the enchantress.

Slowly over the tops of the Ozark Mountains
the moon rose,

Lighting the little tent, and with a mysterious
splendor

Touching the sombre leaves, and embracing
and filling the woodland.

With a delicious sound the brook rushed by,
and the branches

Swayed and sighed overhead in scarcely audi-
ble whispers.

Filled with the thoughts of love was Evange-
line's heart, but a secret,

Subtile sense crept in of pain and indefinite
terror,

As the cold, poisonous snake creeps into the
nest of the swallow.

It was no earthly fear. A breath from the region
of spirits
Seemed to float in the air of night; and she felt
for a moment
That, like the Indian maid, she, too, was pur-
suing a phantom.
With this thought she slept, and the fear and
the phantom had vanished.
❧ Early upon the morrow the march was re-
sumed; and the Shawnee
Said, as they journeyed along, "On the west-
ern slope of these mountains
Dwells in his little village the Black Robe chief
of the Mission.
Much he teaches the people, and tells them of
Mary and Jesus;
Loud laugh their hearts with joy, and weep
with pain, as they hear him."
Then, with a sudden and secret emotion, Evan-
geline answered,
"Let us go to the Mission, for there good tid-
ings await us!"
Thither they turned their steeds; and behind
a spur of the mountains,
Just as the sun went down, they heard a mur-
mur of voices,
And in a meadow green and broad, by the
bank of a river,
Saw the tents of the Christians, the tents of the
Jesuit Mission.
Under a towering oak, that stood in the midst
of the village,
Knelt the Black Robe chief with his children.
A crucifix fastened
High on the trunk of the tree, and overshad-
owed by grape-vines,
Looked with its agonized face on the multitude
kneeling beneath it.

This was their rural chapel. Aloft, through the
intricate arches
Of its aërial roof, arose the chant of their ves-
pers,
Mingling its notes with the soft susurrus and
sighs of the branches.
Silent, with heads uncovered, the travellers,
nearer approaching,
Knelt on the swarded floor, and joined in the
evening devotions.
But when the service was done, and the bene-
diction had fallen
Forth from the hands of the priest, like seed
from the hands of the sower,
Slowly the reverend man advanced to the
strangers and bade them
Welcome; and when they replied, he smiled
with benignant expression,
Hearing the homelike sounds of his mother-
tongue in the forest,
And, with words of kindness, conducted them
into his wigwam.
There upon mats and skins they reposed, and
on cakes of the maize-ear
Feasted, and slaked their thirst from the water
gourd of the teacher.
Soon was their story told; and the priest with
solemnity answered:—
"Not six suns have risen and set since Gabriel,
seated
On this mat by my side, where now the maiden
reposes,
Told me this same sad tale; then arose and
continued his journey!"
Soft was the voice of the priest, and he spake
with an accent of kindness;
But on Evangeline's heart fell his words as in
winter the snow-flakes

Fall into some lone nest from which the birds
    have departed.

"Far to the north he has gone," continued the
    priest; "but in autumn,

When the chase is done, will return again to
    the Mission."

Then Evangeline said, and her voice was meek
    and submissive,

"Let me remain with thee, for my soul is sad
    and afflicted."

So seemed it wise and well unto all; and be-
    times on the morrow,

Mounting his Mexican steed, with his Indian
    guides and companions,

Homeward Basil returned, and Evangeline
    stayed at the Mission.

℀ Slowly, slowly, slowly the days succeeded
    each other,—

Days and weeks and months; and the fields of
    maize that were springing

Green from the ground when a stranger she
    came, now waving above her,

Lifted their slender shafts, with leaves inter-
    lacing, and forming

Cloisters for mendicant crows and granaries
    pillaged by squirrels.

Then in the golden weather the maize was
    husked, and the maidens

Blushed at each blood-red ear, for that beto-
    kened a lover,

But at the crooked laughed, and called it a thief
    in the cornfield.

Even the blood-red ear to Evangeline brought
    not her lover.

"Patience!" the priest would say; "have faith,
    and thy prayer will be answered!

Look at this delicate plant that lifts its head
    from the meadow,

See how its leaves are turned to the north, as
    true as the magnet;

This is the compass-flower, that the finger of
    God has planted

Here in the houseless wild, to direct the travel-
    ler's journey

Over the sea-like, pathless, limitless waste of
    the desert.

Such in the soul of man is faith. The blossoms
    of passion,

Gay and luxuriant flowers, are brighter and
    fuller of fragrance,

But they beguile us, and lead us astray, and
    their odor is deadly.

Only this humble plant can guide us here, and
    hereafter

Crown us with asphodel flowers, that are wet
    with the dews of nepenthe."

❦ So came the autumn, and passed, and the
    winter,—yet Gabriel came not;

Blossomed the opening spring, and the notes
    of the robin and bluebird

Sounded sweet upon wold and in wood, yet
    Gabriel came not.

But on the breath of the summer winds a rumor
    was wafted

Sweeter than song of bird, or hue or odor of
    blossom.

Far to the north and east, it said, in the Michi-
    gan forests,

Gabriel had his lodge by the banks of the Sagi-
    naw river.

And, with returning guides, that sought the
    lakes of St. Lawrence,

Saying a sad farewell, Evangeline went from
    the Mission.

When over weary ways, by long and perilous
    marches,

She had attained at length the depths of the
    Michigan forests,
Found she the hunter's lodge deserted and
    fallen to ruin!
℃ Thus did the long sad years glide on, and in
    seasons and places
Divers and distant far was seen the wandering
    maiden;—
Now in the Tents of Grace of the meek Mo-
    ravian Missions,
Now in the noisy camps and the battle-fields of
    the army,
Now in secluded hamlets, in towns and popu-
    lous cities.
Like a phantom she came, and passed away
    unremembered.
Fair was she and young, when in hope began
    the long journey;
Faded was she and old, when in disappoint-
    ment it ended.
Each succeeding year stole something away
    from her beauty,
Leaving behind it, broader and deeper, the
    gloom and the shadow.
Then there appeared and spread faint streaks
    of gray o'er her forehead,
Dawn of another life, that broke o'er her earth-
    ly horizon,
As in the eastern sky the first faint streaks of
    the morning.

⊱ V ⊰

I<small>N</small> that delightful land which is washed by
 the Delaware's waters,
Guarding in sylvan shades the name of Penn
 the apostle,
Stands on the banks of its beautiful stream the
 city he founded.
There all the air is balm, and the peach is the
 emblem of beauty,
And the streets still re-echo the names of the
 trees of the forest,
As if they fain would appease the Dryads whose
 haunts they molested.
There from the troubled sea had Evangeline
 landed, an exile,

Finding among the children of Penn a home
    and a country.
There old René Leblanc had died; and when
    he departed,
Saw at his side only one of all his hundred
    descendants.
Something at least there was in the friendly
    streets of the city,
Something that spake to her heart, and made
    her no longer a stranger;
And her ear was pleased with the Thee and
    Thou of the Quakers,
For it recalled the past, the old Acadian coun-
    try,
Where all men were equal, and all were broth-
    ers and sisters.
So, when the fruitless search, the disappointed
    endeavor,
Ended, to recommence no more upon earth,
    uncomplaining,
Thither, as leaves to the light, were turned her
    thoughts and her footsteps.
As from a mountain's top the rainy mists of
    the morning
Roll away, and afar we behold the landscape
    below us,
Sun-illumined, with shining rivers and cities
    and hamlets,
So fell the mists from her mind, and she saw
    the world far below her,
Dark no longer, but all illumined with love;
    and the pathway
Which she had climbed so far, lying smooth
    and fair in the distance.
Gabriel was not forgotten. Within her heart
    was his image,
Clothed in the beauty of love and youth, as last
    she beheld him,

Only more beautiful made by his deathlike
  silence and absence.

Into her thoughts of him time entered not, for
  it was not.

Over him years had no power; he was not
  changed, but transfigured;

He had become to her heart as one who is dead,
  and not absent;

Patience and abnegation of self, and devotion
  to others,

This was the lesson a life of trial and sorrow
  had taught her.

So was her love diffused, but, like to some
  odorous spices,

Suffered no waste nor loss, though filling the
  air with aroma.

Other hope had she none, nor wish in life, but
  to follow

Meekly, with reverent steps, the sacred feet of
  her Saviour.

Thus many years she lived as a Sister of Mercy;
  frequenting

Lonely and wretched roofs in the crowded
  lanes of the city,

Where distress and want concealed themselves
  from the sunlight,

Where disease and sorrow in garrets languished
  neglected.

Night after night, when the world was asleep,
  as the watchman repeated

Loud, through the gusty streets, that all was
  well in the city,

High at some lonely window he saw the light
  of her taper.

Day after day, in the gray of the dawn, as slow
  through the suburbs

Plodded the German farmer, with flowers and
  fruits for the market,

Met he that meek, pale face, returning home
    from its watchings.

❡ Then it came to pass that a pestilence fell on
    the city,
Presaged by wondrous signs, and mostly by
    flocks of wild pigeons,
Darkening the sun in their flight, with naught
    in their craws but an acorn.
And, as the tides of the sea arise in the month
    of September,
Flooding some silver stream, till it spreads to
    a lake in the meadow,
So death flooded life, and, o'erflowing its natu-
    ral margin,
Spread to a brackish lake, the silver stream of
    existence.
Wealth had no power to bribe, nor beauty to
    charm, the oppressor;
But all perished alike beneath the scourge of
    his anger; —
Only, alas! the poor, who had neither friends
    nor attendants,
Crept away to die in the almshouse, home of
    the homeless.
Then in the suburbs it stood, in the midst of
    meadows and woodlands; —
Now the city surrounds it; but still, with its
    gateway and wicket
Meek, in the midst of splendor, its humble
    walls seem to echo
Softly the words of the Lord: — "The poor ye
    always have with you."
Thither, by night and by day, came the Sister
    of Mercy. The dying
Looked up into her face, and thought, indeed,
    to behold there
Gleams of celestial light encircle her forehead
    with splendor,

Such as the artist paints o'er the brows of saints
     and apostles,

Or such as hangs by night o'er a city seen at a
     distance.

Unto their eyes it seemed the lamps of the city
     celestial,

Into whose shining gates erelong their spirits
     would enter.

❡ Thus, on a Sabbath morn, through the streets,
     deserted and silent,

Wending her quiet way, she entered the door
     of the almshouse.

Sweet on the summer air was the odor of
     flowers in the garden;

And she paused on her way to gather the fair-
     est among them,

That the dying once more might rejoice in
     their fragrance and beauty.

Then, as she mounted the stairs to the corri-
     dors, cooled by the east wind,

Distant and soft on her ear fell the chimes from
     the belfry of Christ Church,

While, intermingled with these, across the
     meadows were wafted

Sounds of psalms, that were sung by the Swedes
     in their church at Wicaco.

Soft as descending wings fell the calm of the
     hour on her spirit;

Something within her said, "At length thy
     trials are ended";

And, with light in her looks, she entered the
     chambers of sickness.

Noiselessly moved about the assiduous, careful
     attendants,

Moistening the feverish lip, and the aching
     brow, and in silence

Closing the sightless eyes of the dead, and con-
     cealing their faces,

Where on their pallets they lay, like drifts of
  snow by the roadside.
Many a languid head, upraised as Evangeline
  entered,
Turned on its pillow of pain to gaze while she
  passed, for her presence
Fell on their hearts like a ray of the sun on
  the walls of a prison.
And, as she looked around, she saw how Death,
  the consoler,
Laying his hand upon many a heart, had healed
  it forever.
Many familiar forms had disappeared in the
  night-time;
Vacant their places were, or filled already by
  strangers.
℃ Suddenly, as if arrested by fear or a feeling of
  wonder,
Still she stood, with her colorless lips apart,
  while a shudder
Ran through her frame, and, forgotten, the
  flowerets dropped from her fingers,
And from her eyes and cheeks the light and
  bloom of the morning.
Then there escaped from her lips a cry of such
  terrible anguish,
That the dying heard it, and started up from
  their pillows.
On the pallet before her was stretched the
  form of an old man.
Long, and thin, and gray were the locks that
  shaded his temples;
But, as he lay in the morning light, his face
  for a moment
Seemed to assume once more the forms of its
  earlier manhood;
So are wont to be changed the faces of those
  who are dying.

Hot and red on his lips still burned the flush
of the fever,

As if life, like the Hebrew, with blood had
besprinkled its portals,

That the Angel of Death might see the sign,
and pass over.

Motionless, senseless, dying, he lay, and his
spirit exhausted

Seemed to be sinking down through infinite
depths in the darkness,

Darkness of slumber and death, forever sink-
ing and sinking.

Then through those realms of shade, in multi-
plied reverberations,

Heard he that cry of pain, and through the
hush that succeeded

Whispered a gentle voice, in accents tender and
saint-like,

"Gabriel! O my beloved!" and died away into
silence.

Then he beheld, in a dream, once more the
home of his childhood;

Green Acadian meadows, with sylvan rivers
among them,

Village, and mountain, and woodlands; and,
walking under their shadow,

As in the days of her youth, Evangeline rose
in his vision.

Tears came into his eyes; and as slowly he
lifted his eyelids,

Vanished the vision away, but Evangeline knelt
by his bedside.

Vainly he strove to whisper her name, for the
accents unuttered

Died on his lips, and their motion revealed
what his tongue would have spoken.

Vainly he strove to rise; and Evangeline, kneel-
ing beside him,

Kissed his dying lips, and laid his head on her
    bosom.

Sweet was the light of his eyes; but it suddenly
    sank into darkness,

As when a lamp is blown out by a gust of wind
    at a casement.

℃ All was ended now, the hope, and the fear,
    and the sorrow,

All the aching of heart, the restless, unsatisfied
    longing,

All the dull, deep pain, and constant anguish
    of patience!

And, as she pressed once more the lifeless head
    to her bosom,

Meekly she bowed her own, and murmured,
    "Father, I thank thee!"

EPILOGUE

S<small>TILL</small> stands the forest primeval; but far
 away from its shadow,
Side by side, in their nameless graves, the lovers
 are sleeping.
Under the humble walls of the little Catholic
 churchyard,
In the heart of the city, they lie, unknown
 and unnoticed.
Daily the tides of life go ebbing and flowing
 beside them,
Thousands of throbbing hearts, where theirs
 are at rest and forever,
Thousands of aching brains, where theirs no
 longer are busy,

Thousands of toiling hands, where theirs have
    ceased from their labors,
Thousands of weary feet, where theirs have
    completed their journey!
❡ Still stands the forest primeval; but under
    the shade of its branches
Dwells another race, with other customs and
    language.
Only along the shore of the mournful and misty
    Atlantic
Linger a few Acadian peasants, whose fathers
    from exile
Wandered back to their native land to die in
    its bosom.
In the fisherman's cot the wheel and the loom
    are still busy;
Maidens still wear their Norman caps and their
    kirtles of homespun,
And by the evening fire repeat Evangeline's
    story,
While from its rocky caverns the deep-voiced,
    neighboring ocean
Speaks, and in accents disconsolate answers the
    wail of the forest.

THE TEXT OF THIS CENTENNIAL
EDITION HAS BEEN SET IN THE
GRANJON TYPES, AND PRINTED ON
SPECIALLY-MADE PETER PAUPER
PAPER AT MOUNT VERNON, N. Y.